Women of Purpose
Autumn Retreat 2012

" Blessings "

This journal belongs to:

© 2011 by Barbour Publishing, Inc.

Compiled by Marla Tipton.

ISBN 978-1-61626-181-8

Cover and interior design by Koechel Peterson & Associates, Minneapolis, Minnesota

Published by Barbour Publishing, Inc., P.O. Box 719, Uhrichsville, Ohio 44683, www.barbourbooks.com

Our mission is to publish and distribute inspirational products offering exceptional value and biblical encouragement to the masses.

Member of the
Evangelical Christian
Publishers Association

Printed in China.

JOYFUL
blessings

a journal

BARBOUR
PUBLISHING

Cherish all of your happy moments;
they make a fine cushion for old age.

BOOTH TARKINGTON

Each of us may be sure that if God sends us
on stony paths, He will provide us with strong
shoes, and He will not send us out on any
journey for which He does not equip us well.

ALEXANDER MACLAREN

Humor is the great thing, the saving
thing. The minute it crops up, all
irritation and resentments slip away,
and a sunny spirit takes their place.

MARK TWAIN

. . . .

. . . .

. . . .

. . . .

. . . .

. . . .

. . . .

. . . .

. . . .

. . . .

. . . .

. . . .

. . . .

. . . .

. . . .

. . . .

I am beginning to learn that it's the sweet, simple things of life which are the real ones after all.

LAURA INGALLS WILDER

Take me by the hand;

lead me down the path of truth.

PSALM 25:5 MSG

There are no better feelings in life than

the feelings you experience when you

are surrounded by the friends you love.

<small>Unknown</small>

The day is lost in which
one has not laughed.

FRENCH PROVERB

Do not go where the path may lead;
go instead where there is
no path and leave a trail.

RALPH WALDO EMERSON

Now faith is the substance of things hoped for, the evidence of things not seen.

HEBREWS 11:1 KJV

Twenty years from now you will be more
disappointed by the things you didn't do than by
the ones you did do. So throw off the bowlines.
Sail away from the safe harbor. Catch the trade
winds in your sails. Explore. Dream. Discover.

MARK TWAIN

Worrying is like a rocking chair;
it gives you something to do
but doesn't get you anywhere.

UNKNOWN

God has paved our journey

through the adventure of life. . . .

Our friends are the flowers

He has planted along the way.

UNKNOWN

We don't laugh because
we're happy—we're happy
because we laugh.

WILLIAM JAMES

The next time you feel you're riding the saggy-bellied mule of dashed dreams, shift your focus from the destination to the journey. Perhaps God has lessons, gifts, and ministry along the way that will put you on the track to a victorious finish line.

RACHEL ST. JOHN-GILBERT

My soul will be satisfied
as with the richest of
foods; with singing lips
my mouth will praise you.

PSALM 63:5

The cross is the only ladder
high enough to touch the
threshold of heaven.
GEORGE DANA BOARDMAN

Our prayers should be for
blessings in general, for God
knows best what is good for us.

SOCRATES

....

....

....

....

....

....

....

....

....

....

....

....

....

....

....

. . . .

. . . .

. . . .

. . . .

. . . .

. . . .

. . . .

. . . .

. . . .

. . . .

. . . .

. . . .

. . . .

. . . .

. . . .

. . . .

God created you.

He knows you and every aspect of you.

His love for you is boundless,

and His joy in you comes full circle

each time you call Him into your life in prayer.

KAREN MOORE

You pay God a compliment
by asking great things of Him.

TERESA OF AVILA

As we have opportunity,

let us do good to all people.

GALATIANS 6:10

Write it on your heart that
every day is the best day
in the year.

RALPH WALDO EMERSON

Nothing hurts so much as dissatisfaction with our circumstances. . . .
God knows what He is doing, and there is nothing accidental in the
life of the believer. Nothing but good can come to those
who are wholly His.

WATCHMAN NEE

The greatest happiness of
life is the conviction that
we are loved—loved for
ourselves, or rather,
loved in spite of ourselves.

VICTOR HUGO

Imagine God as one who sees only the best in
you. If you hold yourself to that vision of your
own perfection, you will become merciful toward
your faults and will be able to easily correct them.

UNKNOWN

Our Lord has written the promise of
the resurrection, not in books alone,
but in every leaf in springtime.

MARTIN LUTHER

No temptation has seized you except what

is common to man. And God is faithful. . . .

When you are tempted, he will also provide

a way out so that you can stand up under it.

1 Corinthians 10:13

For [God] is, indeed, a wonderful Father
who longs to pour out His mercy upon us,
and whose majesty is so great that He can
transform us from deep within.

TERESA OF AVILA

Our life is full of brokenness—broken relationships, broken promises, broken expectations. How can we live with that brokenness without becoming bitter and resentful except by returning again and again to God's faithful presence in our lives?

HENRI NOUWEN

Above all else, know this:
Be prepared at all times for
the gifts of God and be ready
always for new ones. For God is
a thousand times more ready to
give than we are to receive.

MEISTER ECKHART

. . . .

. . . .

. . . .

. . . .

. . . .

. . . .

. . . .

. . . .

. . . .

. . . .

. . . .

. . . .

. . . .

. . . .

. . . .

. . . .

know what it is to be in need, and I know what it is to have

plenty. I have learned the secret of being content

in any and every situation, whether well fed or hungry,

whether living in plenty or in want.

PHILIPPIANS 4:12

[God] knows everything about us. And He cares about everything. Moreover, He can manage every situation. And He loves us! Surely this is enough to open the wellsprings of joy. . . . And joy is always a source of strength.

HANNAH WHITALL SMITH

An infinite God can give all of Himself to each of His children. He does not distribute Himself that each may have a part, but to each one He gives all of Himself as full as if there were no others.

A. W. TOZER

Love is the greatest thing that God can give us; for He Himself is love; and it is the greatest thing we can give to God.

JEREMY TAYLOR

He who counts the stars and calls them by
their names is in no danger of forgetting
His own children. He knows your case as
thoroughly as if you were the only creature
He ever made, or the only saint He ever loved.

CHARLES SPURGEON

Do not be anxious about anything, but in everything, by prayer and petition, with thanksgiving, present your requests to God.

PHILIPPIANS 4:6

God often comforts us, not by
changing the circumstances of
our lives, but by changing our
attitude toward them.

S. H. B. MASTERMAN

Have confidence in God's
mercy, for when you think
He is a long way from you
He is. . .near
THOMAS À KEMPIS

Your worst days are never so bad that you are beyond

the reach of God's grace. And your best days are never

so good that you are beyond the need for God's grace.

UNKNOWN

If the Lord be with us, we have
no cause of fear. His eye is
upon us, His arm over us,
His ear open to our prayer—
His grace sufficient,
His promise unchangeable.

JOHN NEWTON

"If God gives such attention to the appearance of wildflowers—most of which are never even seen— don't you think he'll attend to you, take pride in you, do his best for you?"

MATTHEW 6:30 MSG

Your Father will hold you in His hand
and shape you according to His will
and purpose as long as you
are willing to let Him.

KAREN MOORE

. . . .

. . . .

. . . .

. . . .

. . . .

. . . .

. . . .

. . . .

. . . .

. . . .

. . . .

. . . .

. . . .

. . . .

. . . .

. . . .

God created us with an overwhelming desire
to soar. . . . He designed us to be tremendously
productive and "to mount up with wings like
eagles," realistically dreaming of what He can
do with our potential.

CAROL KENT

Be the living expression of God's
kindness: kindness in your face,
kindness in your eyes, kindness in
your smile, kindness in
your warm greeting.

MOTHER TERESA

The soul is a temple, and God is
silently building it by night and by
day. Precious thoughts are building
it; unselfish love is building it;
all-penetrating faith is building it.

Henry Ward Beecher

"The joy of the LORD
is your strength.
NEHEMIAH 8:10

ive me a task too big, too hard for human

ands, then I shall come at length to lean on

hee, and leaning, find my strength.

J. H. FOWLER

Praise God for all that is past. Trust Him for all that is to come.

UNKNOWN

A true friend unbosoms freely, advises
justly, assists readily, adventures boldly,
takes all patiently, defends courageously,
and continues a friend unchangeably.

WILLIAM PENN

If you can eat today, enjoy the sunshine today, mix good cheer with friends today, enjoy it and bless God for it.

HENRY WARD BEECHER

The eternal God is your refuge,

and underneath are the everlasting arms.

DEUTERONOMY 33:27

Life itself cannot give you joy
unless you really will it.
Life just gives you time and space—
it's up to you to fill it.

CHINESE PROVERB

Every now and then it's delightful to have
the kind of laugh that makes your stomach
jiggle. . .that sends tears down your face
and causes your eyes to squint so it's
impossible to see!

Unknown

Walking with a friend in the
dark is better than walking
alone in the light

HELEN KELLER

Cheerfulness brings sunshine
to the soul and drives away
the shadows of anxiety.

HANNAH WHITALL SMITH

The friend given you by circumstances over which you have no control was God's own gift.

FREDERICK ROBERTSON

You can be sure that God will take care of everything you need, his generosity exceeding even yours in the glory that pours from Jesus. Our God and Father abounds in glory that just pours out into eternity.

PHILIPPIANS 4:19–20 MSG

It is pleasing to God whenever
you rejoice or laugh from the
bottom of your heart.

MARTIN LUTHER

Bringing joy to a friend is one
of life's greatest pleasures.

Unknown

The art of being happy lies in the power of extracting happiness from common things.

HENRY WARD BEECHER

It's better to have a partner

than go it alone. . . . And if

one falls down, the other helps.

<small>ECCLESIASTES 4:9–10 MSG</small>

When I think upon my God
my heart is so full of joy
that the notes dance and
leap from my pen

JOSEPH HAYDN

After the friendship of God,

a friend's affection is the greatest

treasure here below.

UNKNOWN

It is of immense
importance to learn
to laugh at ourselves.

Katherine Mansfield

Friendship is not created by what
we give but more by what we share.
It makes a whole world of things
easier to bear.

UNKNOWN

May our Lord Jesus Christ. . .
encourage your hearts and strengthen
you in every good deed and word.

2 Thessalonians 2:16–17

No one is useless in this world who

lightens the burdens of it for another.

Charles Dickens

Close friends contribute to our personal growth. They also contribute to our personal pleasure, making the music sound sweeter and the laughter ring louder because they are there.

UNKNOWN

Keep praying, but be thankful
that God's answers are wiser
than your prayers!

WILLIAM CULBERTSON

Teach me, Father, to value
each day, to live, to love
to laugh, to play

KATHI MILL.

. . . .

. . . .

. . . .

. . . .

. . . .

. . . .

. . . .

. . . .

. . . .

. . . .

. . . .

. . . .

. . . .

. . . .

. . . .

. . . .

. . . .

riends love through

ll kinds of weather.

ROVERBS 17:17 MSG

Life is to be fortified by
many friendships.
To love and to be loved
is the greatest happiness
of existence.

<small>SYDNEY SMITH</small>

All of us could take a lesson
from the weather. It pays no
attention to criticism.

UNKNOWN

Nothing is worth more than this day.

JOHANN WOLFGANG VON GOETHE

riendship is made up of little things—

pat on the back, an unexpected phone call,

small gift, a note of thanks, a batch of

hocolate chip cookies. . . .

NKNOWN

Forgive one another as quickly
and thoroughly as God in
Christ forgave you.

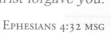

EPHESIANS 4:32 MSG

Just as there comes a warm
sunbeam into every cottage
window, so comes love—born of
God's care for every separate need.

Nathaniel Hawthorne

A friend hears the song in my
heart and sings it to me when
my memory fails.

UNKNOWN

When you get into a tight place and everything goes against you, till it seems as though you cannot hang on a minute longer, never give up then, for that is just the place and time that the tide will turn.

HARRIET BEECHER STOWE

There is no duty we so underrate as the duty of being happy. By being happy, we sow benefits upon the world.

Robert Louis Stevenson

Bless the LORD, O my soul,

and forget not all his benefits.

PSALM 103:2 KJV

A kind heart is a fountain of gladness,

making everything in its vicinity

freshen into smiles.

WASHINGTON IRVING

. . . .

. . . .

. . . .

. . . .

. . . .

. . . .

. . . .

. . . .

. . . .

. . . .

. . . .

. . . .

. . . .

. . . .

. . . .

. . . .

Any child can tell you that the sole

purpose of a middle name is so he

can tell when he's really in trouble.

UNKNOWN

Joy is the net of love by which
you can catch souls.

MOTHER TERESA

He's the stars in the heaven, a smile on some face,
A leaf on a tree or a rose in a vase.
He's winter and autumn and summer and spring,
In short, God is every real and wonderful thing.

HELEN STEINER RICE

We should consider every
day lost in which we have
not danced at least once.

FRIEDRICH NIETZSCHE

···
···
···
···
···
···
···
···
···
···
···
···
···
···
···
···
···
···

*I look behind me and you're there, then up ahead and
you're there, too—your reassuring presence, coming and going.
This is too much, too wonderful—I can't take it all in!*

PSALM 139:5–6 MSG

God meant for us to
have friends. It's His way
of helping us to see the
world through different
eyes than our own.

UNKNOWN

Dear God, there are things we cannot measure

like the depths and waves of sea.

And the heights of stars in heaven

and the joy You bring to me.

HELEN STEINER RICE

Friendship is one of the sweetest joys of
life. Many might have failed beneath
the bitterness of their trial had
they not found a friend.

CHARLES H. SPURGEON

Delight thyself also in the LORD;

and he shall give thee the desires of thine heart.

PSALM 37:14 KJV

Be glad of life, because it gives
you the chance to love, to work,
to play, and to look up at the stars.

<small>Henry Van Dyke</small>

Nothing is ever too hard to do
if your faith is strong and your purpose
is true. . . . So never give up, and never
stop—just journey on to the mountaintop!

HELEN STEINER RICE

To accomplish great things
we must not only act but
also dream; not only plan
but also believe.

ANTOLE FRANCE

A friend is dearer than the light of
heaven, for it would be better for us
that the sun were extinguished than
we should be without friends.

JOHN CHRYSOSTOM

A happy heart makes the face cheerful.

PROVERBS 15:13

There are many things in life that
will catch your eye, but only a few
will catch your heart. Pursue those.

UNKNOWN

I asked God for all things, that I might enjoy life. God gave me life that I might enjoy all things.

UNKNOWN

Celebrate the happiness that friends are always giving;

make every day a holiday and celebrate just living!

Amanda Bradley

Do not be too timid or squeamish. . . .
All life is an experiment. The more
experiments you make, the better.

RALPH WALDO EMERSON

*Be ye glad and rejoice for ever
in that which I create:
for, behold, I create Jerusalem a
rejoicing, and her people a joy.*

Isaiah 65:18 KJV

A true friend never gets in
your way unless you happen
to be going down

ARNOLD GLASOW

Count your age by friends, not years.
Count your life by smiles, not tears.

UNKNOWN

I think I began learning
long ago that those who
are happiest are those who
do the most for others.

BOOKER T. WASHINGTON

Plunge boldly into the thick of
life, and seize it where you will;
it is always interesting.

JOHANN WOLFGANG VAN GOETHE

The Lord has done great things for us,

and we are filled with joy.

PSALM 126:3

To me, every hour of the day and night is an unspeakably perfect miracle.

WALT WHITMAN

In everyone's life, at some time, our inner
fire goes out. It is then burst into flame
by an encounter with another human
being. We should all be thankful for those
people who rekindle the inner spirit.

ALBERT SCHWEITZER

If your heart is full from the blessings God has rained on you lately, revel in this season of joy and let your laughter reverberate to the heavens.

Unknown

A kind heart is a fountain of
gladness, making everything in
its vicinity freshen into smiles.

WASHINGTON IRVING

Blessed be the Lord—

day after day he carries us along.

PSALM 68:19 MSG

If we open the door to let joy walk through,

When we learn to expect the best and most, too,

And believing we'll find a happy surprise

Makes reality out of a fancied surmise.

HELEN STEINER RICE

God's great purpose for the human race [is] that He created us for Himself. This realization of our election by God is the most joyful on earth, and we must learn to rely on this tremendous creative purpose of God.

Oswald Chambers

Add to your joy by counting your blessings. [God] only is the Maker of all things near and far; He paints the wayside flower, He lights the evening star; the wind and waves obey Him, by Him the birds are fed; much more to us, His children, He gives our daily bread.

MATHIAS CLAUDIUS

. . . .

. . . .

. . . .

. . . .

. . . .

. . . .

. . . .

. . . .

. . . .

. . . .

. . . .

. . . .

. . . .

. . . .

. . . .

Never lose an opportunity of seeing anything that

is beautiful; for beauty is God's handwriting—

a wayside sacrament. Welcome it in every fair face,

in every fair sky, in every fair flower,

and thank God for it as a cup of blessing.

RALPH WALDO EMERSON

He has made everything beautiful
in its time.

ECCLESIASTES 3:11

The key to happiness belongs to everyone on earth who recognizes simple things as treasures of great worth. It is impossible to enjoy idling thoroughly unless one has plenty of work to do.

Jerome K. Jerome

He who trusts in the Lord has a diploma for
wisdom granted by inspiration: Happy is he
now, and happier shall he be above

CORRIE TEN BOOM

The sun. . .in its full glory, either at rising or setting—

this, and many other like blessings we enjoy daily;

and for the most of them, because they are so common,

most men forget to pay their praises. But let not us.

Izaak Walton

Do not conform any longer to the pattern of this world, but be transformed by the renewing of your mind.

ROMANS 12:2

. . . .

. . . .

. . . .

. . . .

. . . .

. . . .

. . . .

. . . .

. . . .

. . . .

. . . .

. . . .

. . . .

. . . .

. . . .

. . . .

Love to pray—feel often during the day the
need for prayer, and take trouble to pray.
Prayer enlarges the heart until it is capable
of containing God's gift of Himself.

MOTHER TERESA

Today, allow [God] to search your heart. Ask Him to dig deep. Are there cobwebs that need to be swept out? Things hidden that should be revealed? Let God wash away your anxieties, replacing them with His exceeding great joy!

JANICE HANNA

's a fast-paced world where everyone wants to get

head, Father. Sometimes contentment is frowned upon.

ome folks think of it as laziness or lack of motivation.

ut I know that if I am in the center of Your will, I'll be

ontent. That's the only true contentment there is.

RACHEL QUILLIN

Rest is not idleness, and to lie sometimes
on the grass under trees on a summer's
day, listening to the murmur of the water
or watching the clouds float across the
sky, is by no means a waste of time.

Sir John Lubbock

I value the friend who for me
finds time on his calendar,
but I cherish the friend who for
me does not consult his calendar.

ROBERT BRAULT

Blessed are they who can laugh
at themselves, for they shall
never cease to be amused.

UNKNOWN

. . . .

. . . .

. . . .

. . . .

. . . .

. . . .

. . . .

. . . .

. . . .

. . . .

. . . .

. . . .

. . . .

. . . .

. . . .

. . . .

What matters is not your outer appearance—the styling of your hair, the jewelry you wear, the cut of your clothes— but your inner disposition. Cultivate inner beauty, the gentle, gracious kind that God delights in.

PETER 3:3–4 MSG

If you truly love and enjoy your friends, they are a part of the golden circle that makes life good.

MARJORIE HOLMES

Friends are the angels who lift us
to our feet when our wings have
trouble remembering how to fly.

UNKNOWN

Prayers are the stairs that lead to God,
and there's joy every step of the way
when we make our pilgrimage to Him
with love in our hearts each day.

HELEN STEINER RICE

. . . .

. . . .

. . . .

. . . .

. . . .

. . . .

. . . .

. . . .

. . . .

. . . .

. . . .

. . . .

. . . .

. . . .

. . . .

. . . .

Be still, and know that I am God."

PSALM 46:10

God wants nothing from us except our needs, and these furnish Him with room to display His bounty when He supplies them freely. . . . Not what I have, but what I do not have, is the first point of contact between my soul and God.

CHARLES H. SPURGEON

Where the soul is full of peace
and joy, outward surroundings
and circumstances are of
comparatively little account.

Hannah Whitall Smith

I often think flowers are the
angels' alphabet whereby
they write on hills and fields
mysterious and beautiful
lessons for us to feel and learn

Louisa May Alcott

n all ranks of life the human heart

earns for the beautiful; and the

eautiful things that God makes

re His gift to all alike.

*See! The winter is past;
the rains are over and
gone. Flowers appear on
the earth; the season of
singing has come.*

Song of Solomon 2:11–12

The smallest bit of obedience
opens heaven, and the deepest
truths of God immediately
become ours.

OSWALD CHAMBERS

The thought of You stirs us so deeply
that we cannot be content unless we
praise You, because You have made
us for Yourself and our hearts find no
peace until they rest in You.

AUGUSTINE

leasure is very seldom found where it is

ought. Our brightest blazes are commonly

indled by unexpected sparks.

SAMUEL JOHNSON

God is everything that is good and
comfortable for us. He is our clothing
that for love wraps us, clasps us, and all
surrounds us for tender love.

JULIAN OF NORWICH

Friends come and friends go,
but a true friend sticks by
you like family.

PROVERBS 18:24 MSG

True silence is the rest of
the mind; it is to the spirit
what sleep is to the body,
nourishment and refreshment.

WILLIAM PEN

thing of beauty is a joy forever:

s loveliness increases; it will never pass into nothingness.

JOHN KEATS

There is no duty we so underrate as the duty of being happy. By being happy we sow anonymous benefits upon the world.

ROBERT LOUIS STEVENSON

I still find each day too short for all the thoughts I want
to think, all the walks I want to take, all the books
I want to read, and all the friends I want to see.
The longer I live, the more my mind dwells upon
the beauty and the wonder of the world.

John Burroughs

My heart leaps for joy and I will give thanks to [the LORD] in song.

PSALM 28:7

The best remedy for those who are afraid, lonely,
or unhappy is to go outside, somewhere where they
can be quiet, alone with the heavens, nature, and
God. Because only then does one feel that all is as it
should be and that God wishes to see people happy,
amidst the simple beauty of nature.

ANNE FRANK

There is only one happiness in life,
to love and be loved.

GEORGE SAND

Happiness is as a butterfly, which when
pursued is always beyond your grasp,
but which if you will sit down quietly,
may alight upon you.

NATHANIEL HAWTHORNE

Sometimes your joy is the
source of your smile
but sometimes your smile
can be the source of your joy

THICH NHAT HANH

Before the mountains were born or you

brought forth the earth and the world,

from everlasting to everlasting you are God.

PSALM 90:2

The sea of joy grows best
in a field of peace.

ROBERT J. WICKS

Success is not the key to happiness.
Happiness is the key to success. If you love
what you are doing, you will be successful.

ALBERT SCHWEITZER

Consider the postage stamp:
its usefulness consists in the ability
to stick to one thing till it gets there.

JOSH BILLINGS

. . . .

. . . .

. . . .

. . . .

. . . .

. . . .

. . . .

. . . .

. . . .

. . . .

. . . .

. . . .

. . . .

. . . .

Happiness cannot be traveled to, owned,
earned, worn, or consumed. Happiness is the
spiritual experience of living every minute
with love, grace, and gratitude.

DENIS WAITLEY

God. . .doesn't play hide-and-seek
with us. He's not remote; he's near.

ACTS 17:27 MSG

Getting what you go after is
success; but liking it while you
are getting it is happiness.

BERTHA DAMON

We could never learn to be
brave and patient if there
were only joy in the world

HELEN KELLER

Gratefulness is the key to a happy life that we hold in our hands, because if we are not grateful, then no matter how much we have we will not be happy—because we will always want to have something else or something more.

BROTHER DAVID STEINDL-RAST

Wisdom will enter your heart, and knowledge will be pleasant to your soul.

PROVERBS 2:10

Occasionally in life there are moments. . .
which cannot be completely explained by words.
Their meaning can only be articulated by the
inaudible language of the heart.

MARTIN LUTHER KING JR.

Every great dream begins with a
dreamer. Always remember, you have
within you the strength, the patience,
and the passion to reach for the stars
to change the world.

HARRIET TUBMAN

. . . .

. . . .

. . . .

. . . .

. . . .

. . . .

. . . .

. . . .

. . . .

. . . .

. . . .

. . . .

. . . .

. . . .

. . . .

. . . .

The gloom of the world is but a shadow.

Behind it, yet within our reach, is joy.

There is radiance and glory in the darkness,

could we but see; and to see, we have only to look.

Fra Giovanni Gocondo

Although the world is full of suffering,
it is full also of the overcoming of it.

HELEN KELLER

God is our clothing that wraps,
clasps, and encloses us so as to
never leave us.

JULIAN OF NORWICH

Watch the way you talk. . .

Say only what helps

each word a gift

EPHESIANS 4:29 MSG

Most of us, swimming against the tides of

trouble the world knows nothing about,

need only a bit of praise or encouragement—

and we will make the goal.

JEROME FLEISHMAN

The most spectacular answers
to prayer have come when
I was so helpless, so out of
control as to be able to do
nothing at all for myself.

CATHERINE MARSHALL

I believe that God is in me as the sun is in the
color and fragrance of a flower—the Light in my
darkness, the Voice in my silence.

HELEN KELLER

Just start to sing as you tackle the thing

that "cannot be done" and you'll do it.

EDGAR A. GUEST

....

....

....

....

....

....

....

....

....

....

....

....

....

....

....

Commit to the LORD whatever you do,

and your plans will succeed.

PROVERBS 16:3

As you fall asleep, think of just how much God loves you. Build your faith by recalling all He has done for you. Count your blessings instead of sheep; then sleep peacefully in your heavenly Father's protective arms.

UNKNOWN

Today Jesus is working just as many wonderful works as when He created the heavens and the earth. His wondrous grace, His wonderful omnipotence, is for His child who needs Him and who trusts Him, even today.

CHARLES E. HURLBURT AND T. C. HORTON

Faith does not mean believing
without evidence. It means
believing in realities that go
beyond sense and sight—
for which a totally different
sort of evidence is required.

JOHN BAILLIE

Open wide the windows of our spirits and
fill us full of light; open wide the door of our
hearts, that we may receive and entertain
Thee with all our powers of adoration.

CHRISTINA ROSSETTI

There is a time for everything. . .a time to weep and a time to laugh.

ECCLESIATES 3:1, 4

How can I doubt my worth in Your eyes, Father? You know the number of hairs on my head. You created me, and You said that Your creation is very good. When I'm tempted to get down on myself, remind me that I am special to You, and there's no one just like me.

RACHEL QUILLIN

Make time for laughter with your girlfriends every day. Squeeze the joy out of every moment.

UNKNOWN

. . . .

. . . .

. . . .

. . . .

. . . .

. . . .

. . . .

. . . .

. . . .

. . . .

. . . .

. . . .

. . . .

. . . .

. . . .

You know you've made a new friend when. . .
the differences you find only make the other
person seem more interesting.

ELLYN SANNA

Always laugh when you can.
It is cheap medicine.

LORD BYRON

"*Nothing is impossible with God.*"

LUKE 1:37

Friends help us to live life to
the fullest by making ordinary
days an adventure

UNKNOWN

Today, may you experience something

that reminds you that angels are

watching over you.

Let us not hurry so in our pace of living that we lose sight of the art of living.

SIR FRANCIS BACON

Nothing touches my life that hasn't first passed
through the hand of God. He knows what is best
for me. I will trust His hand in my life, believing
that He sees how all things work together.

UNKNOWN

For the Lord is our salvation
and our strength in every fight,
Our redeemer and protector,
our eternal guiding light.

HELEN STEINER RICE

For this is what the Lord says: . . . "As a mother comforts her child, so will I comfort you. . . ." When you see this, your heart will rejoice and you will flourish like grass; the hand of the Lord will be made known to his servants, but his fury will be shown to his foes.

ISAIAH 66:12–14

His love knows no exceptions,
so never feel excluded—
No matter who or what you are,
your name has been included.

HELEN STEINER RICE

All we really ever need is faith
as a grain of mustard seed,
For all God asks is that you believe.
For if you do, ye shall receive.

HELEN STEINER RICE

After the winter comes the spring
To show us again that in everything
There's always a renewal divinely planned,
Flawlessly perfect, the work of God's hand

HELEN STEINER RICE

He giveth power to the faint; and to them that have no might he increaseth strength. Even the youths shall faint and be weary, and the young men shall utterly fall: but they that wait upon the LORD shall renew their strength; they shall mount up with wings as eagles; they shall run, and not be weary; and they shall walk, and not faint.

ISAIAH 40:29–31 KJV

God cannot give us a
happiness and peace apart
from Himself, because it is
not there. There is no
such thing.

C. S. Lewis

How often we look upon God as our last and
feeblest resource! We go to Him because we
have nowhere else to go. And then we learn
that the storms of life have driven us,
not upon the rocks, but into the desired haven.

George MacDonald

Our Creator would never have made
such lovely days, and have given us
the deep hearts to enjoy them, above
and beyond all thought, unless we
were meant to be immortal.

NATHANIEL HAWTHORNE

[God's] mercy hath no relation to time,

no limitation in time; it is not first, nor last,

but eternal, everlasting.

John Donne

Since God assured us, "I'll never let you
down, never walk off and leave you,"
we can boldly quote, God is there, ready
to help; I'm fearless no matter what.
Who or what can get to me?

HEBREWS 13:5–6 MSG

Be not dismayed whate'er betide,

God will take care of you;

Beneath His wings of love abide,

God will take care of you.

Civilla D. Martin

Thank God then if you have
been led by a rough road. It is
this which has given you your
experience of God's greatness
and lovingkindness.

CHARLES SPURGEON

God left the world unfinished;

the pictures unpainted, the songs unsung,

and the problems unsolved, that man

might know the joys of creation.

Thomas S. Monson

The greatest honor we can give God is to live gladly because of the knowledge of His love.

JULIAN OF NORWICH

....
....
....
....
....
....
....
....
....
....
....
....
....
....
....
....
....
....

Surely he hath borne our griefs, and carried our
sorrows: . . . . But he was wounded for our
transgressions, he was bruised for our iniquities:
the chastisement of our peace was upon him;
and with his stripes we are healed.

Isaiah 53:4–5 KJV

There is nothing but God's grace.
We walk upon it; we breathe it;
we live and die by it; it makes the
nails and axles of the universe.

ROBERT LOUIS STEVENSON

Walk boldly and wisely. . . .

There is a hand above that will help you on.

PHILIP JAMES BAILEY

He sees our little faith and still does not reject it, small as it is. He does not in every case measure out His gifts by the degree of our faith, but by the sincerity and trueness of faith.

CHARLES SPURGEON

....
....
....
....
....
....
....
....
....
....
....
....
....
....
....
....
....

Ye fearful saints fresh courage take;

The clouds ye so much dread

Are big with mercy and shall break

In blessings on your head.

WILLIAM COWPER

"I, your GOD, have a firm grip
on you and I'm not letting go.
I'm telling you, 'Don't panic.
I'm right here to help you.'"

ISAIAH 41:13 MSG

God wants nothing from us except our needs, and these furnish Him with room to display His bounty when He supplies them freely. . . . Not what I have, but what I do not have, is the first point of contact between my soul and God.

CHARLES SPURGEON

So kneel in prayer in His presence,

And you'll find no need to speak;

For softly in quiet communion,

God grants you the peace that you seek.

HELEN STEINER RICE

He's the stars in the heaven, a smile on some face,

A leaf on a tree or a rose in a vase.

He's winter and autumn and summer and spring,

In short, God is every real and wonderful thing.

HELEN STEINER RICE

Thy faithfulness is unto all generations:
thou hast established the earth,
and it abideth.

PSALM 119:90 KJV

You have to know Jesus to delight in His presence,
just as you cannot enjoy a friend until you come to know
each other and enjoy companionship. But knowing and
loving God brings us, His children, joy in His presence
and the prospect of undefined pleasure at His side.
Are you prepared to share those joys with Jesus for eternity?

Pamela McQuade

Every moment is full of wonder,
and God is always present. We have a
Father in heaven who is almighty, who
loves His children as He loves His only
begotten Son, and whose very joy and
delight it is to. . .help them at all times
and under all circumstances.

GEORGE MUELLER

Whether sixty or sixteen, there is in every human being's heart the love of wonder, the sweet amazement at the stars and starlike things, the undaunted challenge of events, the unfailing childlike appetite for what-next, and the joy of the game of living.

SAMUEL ULLMAN

When trials come your way, God will [draw
you close to His heart]. If life is always going
smoothly, comfort is meaningless; but when
you're in the midst of trouble, He comes
alongside with tender love that overflows
your trials and reaches out to others.

PAMELA MCQUADE

Words cannot express the joy which a friend imparts; they only can know who have experienced. A friend is dearer than the light of heaven, for it would be better for us that the sun were extinguished than that we should be without friends.

JOHN CHRYSOSTOM

Yet the LORD longs to be
gracious to you; he rises
to show you compassion.
For the LORD is a God
of justice. Blessed are
all who wait for him!

ISAIAH 30:18

Knowing God is not about what we do, but about whom we love. Our good works mean little if we disconnect from Him. Spend time being still with God today, and a deepened knowledge of Him will be your blessing.

PAMELA McQUADE

I know You want the best for me, Lord,
and You will provide it. My job is to
live my life in a way that glorifies You.
Everything beyond that is a blessing.
I choose to be content.

UNKNOWN

Surely joy will rise up in your soul
as you watch God at work.

Janice Hanna

Happy is the one who has learned to hold the things of this world with a loose grip. Of all classes and descriptions of persons on this earth, they are the happiest of whom it may be said that the thing most hoped for by them are the things not seen.

MENNONITE WRITINGS

When I consider thy heavens, the work of thy fingers, the moon and the stars, which thou hast ordained; what is man, that thou art mindful of him? and the son of man, that thou visitest him? For thou hast made him a little lower than the angels, and hast crowned him with glory and honour.

PSALM 8:3–5 KJV